Sio

The Inspirational Story of Hockey Superstar Sidney Crosby

presentation of the information is without contract or any type of guarantee assurance.

The trademarks that are used are without any consent, and the publication of the trademark is without permission or backing by the trademark owner. All trademarks and brands within this book are for clarifying purposes only and are the owned by the owners themselves, not affiliated with this document.

Table Of Contents

Introduction

As the title already implies, this is a short book about [The Inspirational Story of Hockey Superstar Sidney Crosby] and how he rose from his life in Nova Scotia, Canada to becoming one of today's leading and most-respected hockey players. In his rise to superstardom, Sidney has inspired not only the youth, but fans of all ages throughout the world.

This book also portrays the struggles that Sidney has had to overcome during his early childhood years, his teen years, and up until he became who he is today. A notable source of inspiration is Sidney's service to the community and his strong connection with the fans of the sport. He continues to serve as a humble, fun-loving superstar in a sport that greatly needs it.

Combining incredible offensive creativity, a powerful lower body, a ferocious attacking style, and high hockey IQ, Sidney has shown the ability to completely take over a game. From being a young boy who's family struggled to pay for his hockey gear to becoming one of the greatest hockey players of his generation, you'll learn here how this man has risen to the ranks of the best hockey players today.

Thanks again for grabbing this book. Hopefully you can take some of the examples and lessons from Sidney's story and apply them to your own life!

Chapter 1:

Youth & Family Life

Sidney Patrick Crosby was welcomed into the world on August 7th, 1987. He was born in Halifax, Nova Scotia, Canada, to parents Troy and Trina Crosby, and was followed by a younger sister named Taylor. Sidney was raised in the town of Cole Harbour, about thirty minutes from Halifax by car. Trina worked at a grocery store and Troy worked at a law firm.

Sidney was born into an athletic family, as his father was a goaltender. The elder Crosby was a member of the Dartmouth Moosehead Mounties of the Nova Scotia Senior Hockey League (NSSHL). He was later selected in the 20th round of the Quebec Major Junior Hockey League (QMJHL) Entry Draft. He was drafted 218th overall by the Verdun Junior Canadiens before the 1983-84 season.

Troy spent two seasons with the Junior Canadiens before the National Hockey League came knocking. He was good enough to be drafted by the Montreal Canadiens with the 240th overall selection during the 1984 NHL Draft, but was never able to play at the NHL level. He did play in the 1985 Memorial Cup.

After retiring, Troy returned to Cole Harbour in Nova Scotia where he raised his family. But even though Troy hung up his skates, the desire to play never left him. Seeing his son succeed in the sport closest to his heart is a consolation of sorts for the now-49 year old former goaltender. The proud father of a hockey sensation, Troy's son is an extension of him out there on the ice.

In addition to the skills, the passion for the sport of hockey was passed down from father to son. Young Sidney was a fan of the Canadiens, but his favorite player in the NHL was Steve Yzerman of the Detroit Red Wings. Sidney picked the sport up almost as early as he could walk. By the age of two, he could be found all alone in the family's basement, shooting a puck into the clothes dryer.

Story has it that young Sidney severely damaged the dryer. Realizing his son's penchant for hockey, Troy brought Sidney, then two and a half years old, to a program that taught skating to children with the help of their parents. Father and son would practice once a week. Thanks to his family's help, Sidney was able to skate by the age of three.

Hockey was not the only sport of interest for Sidney. He also played other sports, particularly baseball. But Sidney's family mostly supported his early interest in hockey. He started playing at the age of five when he was part of the Tim Hortons Tim Bits program.

Sidney's potential became noticeable when he was six years old. At that age, he was already playing against nine and ten year olds. The most striking part is that he played well against the older kids. Because of this, Sidney's parents decided to enroll him in a local league (Cole Harbour Wings Minor Hockey Association) while he was still in his early childhood, particularly from novice to the bantam levels. Trina even worked extra jobs in order to have enough funds to buy Sidney's equipment. Before long, Sidney's parents' hard work and sacrifice was paying dividends.

At the ripe old age of seven, Sidney was interviewed by a local newspaper because of his spectacular abilities on the ice. Not long afterwards, he was drawing attention from around Nova Scotia, and then the rest of Canada. The combination of outside approval combined with the continuous support of his parents, allowed Sidney to attend a multitude of hockey camps during his youth. This constant process of refining his skill-set and learning strategy kept Sidney ahead of his peers. At the age of ten,

Sydney scored almost 160 goals in just 55 games in his youth league season.

Sidney tried out for the Dartmouth Subways, but wasn't allowed to play even after making the major midget league team. With a league composed of mostly sixteen and seventeen year old hockey players, thirteen year old Sidney was deemed too young. Sidney returned to play for Cole Harbour's bantam team. A year later, Sidney was finally allowed to play for Dartmouth. Sidney quickly showed the league what they missed out on the year prior.

He scored 217 points to help the Subways reach second place in the Air Canada Cup. His excellent performance got the attention of the media and he was invited to the Canadian Broadcasting Corporation's Hockey day. Now dubbed as "The Next One" by the media, Sidney gave everyone a show when he led the Subways to the National Championships by scoring 27 points in just six games. Even though he and his team lost their final game, his reputation as a hockey phenom was cemented.

Sidney also handled business in the class room, being a straight A student during his junior high school years. He attended Astral Drive Junior High School where his vice-principal said that Sidney was "an amazing role model" who was not only kind to his classmates, but also to "special needs kids". For an early teenage boy to be given such high praise showed that Sidney's maturity has always been one of his strengths.

By the end of his last year at Astral Drive Junior High School, Sidney was deemed a "prodigy" by the national media of Canada. He played for Triple A Midget in 2002 and scored a total of 44 goals in only 31 contests - against players who were between two and three years older than he was. At this point, scouts around the world were drooling at the opportunity to snag the young prospect before anyone else could. Despite not even playing a game in the junior leagues yet, Sidney was predicted to be an NHL player one day.

At the age of fifteen, Sidney enrolled in Shattuck-Saint Mary's. The school was in Faribault, Minnesota and was well-known for it's superb hockey program, which is now also referred to as the "Hogwarts of Hockey". The 18-time USA Hockey National Champs then featured future NHL players Jonathan Toews and Zach Parise.

Sydney would use the time at Shattuck-Saint Mary's to develop his skills, away from the spotlight that was building up around him in Canada. This move was also seen as an opportunity for the young Sidney to mature and develop as a person. He was able to put some muscle on his body and mentally develop as a hockey player.

The team went on to win the US National Championship title during his year there. He was an instrumental part of the team's success, scoring 72 goals in the games he played for Shattuck-St. Marys. Additionally, Sidney showed his athletic versatility when he became one of the school's best pitchers for the baseball team.

At Shattuck-Saint Mary's, Sidney was able to develop a close friendship with another future NHL player, Jack Johnson. The two became best friends and built a competitive relationship where they would constantly push each other to become better hockey players and better overall athletes. In hindsight, the duo was able to build each other's confidence, skill-sets, and prepare each other for hockey at the the highest level. The two kept their relationship strong over the years and are still great friends till this day.

After his year at Shattuck-Saint Mary's, Sidney and his family decided it would be best to return to Canada to continue his development. Sidney had reached the point where he needed to compete with elite competition on a daily basis so that he would not plateau as a hockey player.

He joined the Rimouski Oceanic of the Quebec Major Junior Hockey League as the first overall pick of the 2003 Midget Draft. Sidney scored eight points in his first exhibition game in the league. This quickly earned him the adulation of many, particularly his teammates who started calling him "Darryl" after the former NHL star who once scored ten points in a game -- Darryl Sittler. Sidney followed up with one goal and a couple of assists in his first regular season game.

He totaled 135 points in his first season, including 54 goals scored. Sidney also had 81 assists in 59 games. During his first year in the QMJHL, Sidney earned multiple Player of the Week honors (six), and Player of the Month honors (three). He was also named the Canadian Hockey League (CHL) Player of the Week thrice.

He ended up with the Jean Beliveau Trophy, as the league's top point-scorer. He also took home the RDS/JVC Trophy as the Rookie of the Year, as well as the Michel Briere Memorial Trophy, as the Most Valuable Player in the league. This marked the first time in the league's history that a player won all three awards in the same season – his rookie season at that. On top of all these, Sidney was named Personality of the Year.

The Oceanic won 34 games to get the top spot in the Eastern Division standings. They received a bye in the first round of the playoffs. The team won over the Shawinigan Cataractes in the quarterfinals before bowing out of contention in the semis, courtesy of the Moncton Wildcats. In the nine games the team played in the playoffs, Sidney scored a total of sixteen points. He had seven goals and nine assists as well.

Sidney's impressive season in the QMJHL earned him an invitation to play for the Canadian Junior Hockey Team. At the time of his selection, Sidney was the only player on the team who was under eighteen years of age. The selection also made him only the fifth hockey player to ever represent Team Canada at the age of sixteen. The other four were Jay Bouwmeester, Jason Spezza, Eric Lindos, and "The Great One" Wayne Gretzky.

Sidney played for the team at the 2003 Under-18 Junior World Cup held in the Czech Republic and Slovenia. Team Canada failed to secure the gold for the first time in eight consecutive years. In fact, they failed to win a medal after losing to the Czech Republic in the bronze medal game.

The United States team went on to bag the gold for the nation's first ever title in the tournament, at the expense of Team Russia. Sidney collected four goals for a total of six points during the tournament. He also played for the Nova Scotia team in the 2003 Canada Games, and was named the team captain.

Soon after, Sidney went on to represent his country in two other installments of the World Junior Championships. In the 2004 under-20 tournament, Sidney officially became the youngest player to ever score a goal at the World Junior Championships after scoring in a game against Switzerland, which they won 7 to 2. He was only sixteen years, four months and 21 days old at the time. Finland's Aleksander Barkov later broke the record in 2012, beating Sidney by 21 days. Sidney finished with two goals and three assists to help Team Canada reach a silver medal finish in the tournament.

During this time, the NHL was in a quandary. The labor dispute prevented what was supposed to be the 2004-05 season from taking place. As a response to the potential NHL lockout, another professional hockey league, the World Hockey Association or WHA, was announced.

The WHA was originally a North American professional hockey league that competed with the NHL in the 70s. Among the hockey legends who at one time in their careers played in the WHA were Gordie Howe, Andre Lacroix, Anders Hedberg, Vaclav Nedomansky, Bobby Hull, Ulf Nilsson, Mark Howe, Wayne Gretzky, and Mark Messier.

The proposed modern version of the league went full throttle during the lockout. It started with an Entry Draft that saw Sidney getting picked first overall by Toronto. The WHA also started offering huge contracts to numerous NHL stars as well as a number of up-and-comers. One of them was Sidney.

Another team, Hamilton, offered Sidney a three-year contract worth $7.5 million. He declined the offer citing that he wasn't ready to take the next step. His decision to turn down money and instead further develop his skills turned out to be a blessing in disguise for the phenomenal junior player. WHA never materialized as a professional league after numerous setbacks owing to its instability.

After his eventful experience on the world stage, Sidney returned to the QMJHL for the 2004-05 season, his second with Rimouski. He continued his progression as one of the best young offensive prospects in the world, as he scored 66 goals, 168 points, and recorded 102 assists in 62 games. He showed amazing control of the puck and displayed a number of dazzling offensive moves throughout the season.

At this point, professional scouts were drawing comparisons in Sidney's game to the legendary Wayne Gretzky and Bobby Orr. Sidney finished the year with another Beliveau Trophy and was a no-brainer as the league's Most Valuable Player, Offensive Player of the Year, and Personality of the Year.

Sidney's continuing development and personal accomplishments weren't the only feel good story for the organization. Sidney's success on the ice translated into team success. The Oceanic finished the regular season with the best overall record by winning 45 games and even posted a winning streak of twenty-eight games, which still stands as the longest win streak in the history of the league.

Rimouski finished with only two defeats during the playoffs. The team went on to win the President's Cup, after defeating the Halifax Mooseheads in the final game. Sidney led all players in the playoffs with a total of 31 points, 14 goals and 17 assists, all in just thirteen games. His excellent play garnered him the Guy Lafleur Trophy as the Most Valuable Player of the post-season.

The victory in the QMJHL championship game earned the Oceanic a spot in the 2005 Memorial Cup. The Memorial Cup is regarded as Canada's major tournament at the junior level. The Oceanic were able to make it all the way to the final game before eventually losing to the London Knights by a score of 4-0. Despite a disappointing end to the season, Sidney went on to be named a member of the Tournament All-Star Team and was awarded the Ed Chynoweth Trophy as the entire tournament's leading scorer with eleven points, including six goals and five assists.

Notably impressive in Sidney's time with Oceanic was his ability to hold his own on the ice. There were numerous times when defenders would try to bully him or inflict harm whenever the chance arose. However, Sidney did not fear the corners and was willing to give the punishment right back to anybody who dared try to check him. Because he was such a phenom, he carried a target on his back in each game that he played in. However, by the end of his second season with Oceanic, defenders were aware that they couldn't get into Sidney's head, furthering his respect amongst his peers.

Sidney was again chosen to be part of Canada's national team. He represented the country at the 2005 World Junior Championships held in Grand Forks, North Dakota and Thief River Falls in Minnesota. His six goals and three assists were enough to help Team Canada finally win the gold medal.

Of course, it helped a lot that his teammates included tournament MVP Patrice Bergeron, All-Stars Dion Phaneuf, Jeff Carter, Clarke MacArthur, and Andrew Ladd, among others. To this day, Sidney considers the World Junior Championship win as the most unforgettable moment of his career.

After such a successful season on the ice and with his confidence at an all-time high, Sidney decided that he would be best served to join the 2005 NHL Entry Draft. He attended the combine and was able to show off his measurables to potential teams. However, many scouts reported that Sidney's maturity, personality, and overall confidence was the most impressive aspect of his combine showing, even more than his obvious skills on the ice.

Chapter 2:

Professional Life

As the 2005 NHL Draft neared, it was being regarded by some as the "Sidney Crosby Sweepstakes" because there was no doubt that the team that finished with the top pick would select Sidney. Furthermore, he was all but guaranteed to be a franchise changing player for whichever team that drafted him.

Similar to LeBron James of the NBA just two years prior, Sidney's entrance into his sport's draft had been anticipated for multiple years before he was even eligible.

But the 2005 NHL Draft was not the typical draft. As mentioned earlier, a lockout prevented what was supposed to be the 2004-05 season. Because the 88th NHL season was non-existent, there was no way of figuring out the draft order, much less the lottery. The NHL decided to go through with a weighted lottery. The performances of all the teams in the previous four seasons were used to determine the lottery.

Nine days prior to the draft, it was determined that the Pittsburgh Penguins would have the first selection. Sidney had already developed a relationship with aging star, Mario Lemieux, and was ready to join the organization on draft night. After only a few weeks from the day the Penguins organization publicly announced that they would select Sidney, they had already sold more tickets than they did in the entire previous year.

Sidney was drafted on July 30th, 2005. Not long afterwards, he and the Penguins agreed to a $10 million deal that spanned three years, which was the maximum for a rookie salary at the time. The contract also contained performance-based bonuses.

Sidney's NHL debut came in early October of 2005, when the team faced the New Jersey Devils. He posted an assist during his first career game and scored his first goal three days later against the Boston Bruins in the Penguins' home opener. He also went on to register two assists in the same game, totaling three points. By the end of his first month, Sidney had scored two goals and dished out twelve assists in only eleven games, earning him the NHL's "Rookie of the Month" honor.

Sidney continued his impressive play as the season progressed. An unexpected end to Mario

Lemieux's career came after only twenty-six games into the year's schedule. Due to an irregular heartbeat, it was determined by doctors that Lemieux would be best served to end his career immediately.

This was the second time that the Hall of Famer was forced to retire. In 1997, he hung up his skates after battling back problems and Hodgkin's lymphoma. He came out of retirement in 2000 and partnered with old friend Jaromir Jagr once more to lead the Penguins to several successful seasons.

Though 2006 marked the last time Lemieux would play on the ice as a professional, he continued to support the Penguins, especially Sidney. In fact, Sidney stayed with Lemieux and his family during the season. He was not only part of the Penguins family, Sidney was "adopted" by the Lemieux family as their own.

As the midway point of the season neared, the Penguins players experienced another unexpected event. Head Coach Ed Olczyk was fired in exchange for Michel Therrien in mid-December. In Therrien's second day on the job, he appointed Sidney as the alternate captain of the team - a great honor for a rookie player. As expected, there was criticism from the outside, mainly from "experts" who felt that Sidney was not qualified enough for the title. Nonetheless, the club proceeded and made it through all of the drama of the coaching change and Sidney's new designation.

After a tough year with many ups and downs, the Penguins finished with the worst record in the entire Eastern Conference, showing that they had not improved much from the previous year. However, the loss of Lemieux's leadership and a coaching change mid-season certainly did not set them up for short-term success. Despite the poor performance as a team, Sidney had a successful first campaign as an NHL player.

He set franchise records in points (102) and assists (63) for a rookie, breaking the ones previously set by Lemieux. He also became the youngest player in NHL history to record 100 total points in a single season, as well as the seventh rookie to ever accomplish the feat. Not only was Sidney one of the best players on the Penguins, but he was also considered one of the best young offensive players in the game. Additionally, Sidney finished the year sixth in the NHL in scoring and seventh in assists.

In almost any other season, Sidney would have been awarded the Calder Memorial Trophy as the League's Rookie of the Year. However, because of the greatly-hyped and ultra-talented Alexander Ovechkin of the Washington Capitals, Sidney came in second place in the voting. He also finished second to Ovechkin in total points among rookies.

Even though Sidney showed noticeable signs of potential in his rookie season, he also struggled to adjust to some facets of the game. The physicality was greater than anything he had dealt with before, with many defenders trying to rough Sidney up whenever they could. Furthermore, he found it difficult to score goals at the beginning of the year, as he became acclimated to playing on the wing for the Penguins.

During the offseason, Sidney again plied his wares for Team Canada in the World Junior Championships. He scored a total of eight goals, the most during the tournament. He also had 16 points, further cementing his claim as the youngest player to win the WJC scoring title. His offensive exploits, however, were not enough to lead Team Canada back to the top of the podium. They finished fourth overall after losing to Finland in the bronze medal game.

Sidney and the Penguins entered the next season with higher expectations, hoping to build on the previous year's chemistry and develop their young talent even further. Sidney was the target of many defenders once again and was forced into a large leadership role for the team. All of this responsibility was handled well on Sidney's part and he was able to keep the team within striking distance of the playoffs by mid-season.

Sidney's first half of the season included a hat trick against the Philadelphia Flyers in late October and a six point game against them in mid-December. After the second game against the Flyers, Sidney jumped into the NHL scoring lead and was able to maintain it for the rest of the year. Upon season's end, Sidney had totaled 36 goals, 120 points, and 84 assists in only 79 games - making him the first teenager to lead the league in scoring since Wayne Gretzky did it more than twenty-five years prior.

As a team, the Penguins grew along with Sidney. Their second season saw an improvement in record, as well as resilience and effort. The other players around Sidney were also developing their individual games simultaneously, including Evgeni Malkin and Jordan Staal. All of these factors, along with the team buying into Coach Therrien's philosophies, catapulted the Penguins from last place in the Eastern Conference to making a playoff appearance in the Stanley Cup Playoffs. They finished fifth in the standings and were met by the Ottawa Senators in the first round.

The inexperienced Penguins fought hard but eventually lost the opening round to Ottawa, who was the eventual runner-up in the tournament. Even though the season ended on a disappointing note, there was no doubt that the franchise was moving in the right direction, as they headed into an off-season with much to look forward to. For the series, Sidney finished with five points, including a scored goal in his playoff debut. Sidney was ready to rest when the offseason came, as he had been playing for more than a month with a broken bone in one of his feet.

After the Penguins' season ended, Sidney was appointed as the team's captain. At only nineteen years of age, he became the youngest team captain in NHL history. He accepted the appointment humbly, after having denied the position during the season because he didn't feel he was quite ready. Nonetheless, Sidney's coaches and teammates saw him as a leader and very mature for his age.

Sidney's work ethic and dedication to playing a team game earned the respect of his teammates much sooner than the typical sports phenom. The fact that he did not desire any unnecessary attention and worked as hard as anybody on the team, made his accomplishments even that much more admirable. Just like most other times in Sidney's hockey career, he would need to accept a big responsibility at a younger age than any of his peers.

Following the season, Sidney was awarded the triple crown of NHL awards, receiving the Hart Memorial Trophy, the Lester B. Pearson Award, and the Art Ross Trophy. It made Sidney the youngest player to ever win the Lester B.

Pearson Award and the second youngest to win the Hart Memorial Trophy. His honor as the Lester B. Pearson Award winner signaled a great respect for Sidney around the league, because voting for the award was done by his peers. He was also named to the NHL's First All-Star Team, becoming the youngest player to ever receive the honor.

As Sidney entered the 2007-08 season, Penguins' management decided to lock him up for the foreseeable future. He and the team agreed to a $43.5 million contract extension that spanned five years on July 10th, 2007. He continued just where he'd left off the previous season, averaging around three points for every two games played. He also recorded a Gordie Howe hat trick against the Boston Bruins by the mid-season mark - the rare feat includes a player scoring a goal, assisting on a goal, and getting into a fight. The fight was the first of Sidney's NHL career.

After being named to the 2008 All-Star Game as a starter, Sidney suffered an unfortunate high ankle sprain just a few weeks later. The injury was caused by crashing into the boards leg first. It forced Sidney to miss the All-Star festivities. He went on to miss a total of twenty-one games and did not make a return to the team until a March 4th match-up against the Tampa Bay Lighting. After realizing that he was not fully healed, Sidney and the team decided that he should sit out a little longer. After taking the next seven games off, Sidney made his next return on March 27th.

Sidney's injury served as a blessing in disguise for the Penguins, allowing his teammates to take on bigger roles that would further their development. The most notable improvement was seen from Evgeni Malkin, who was slowly becoming a dominant force in the league. Despite being in only his second season, Malkin took over the majority of Sidney's scoring responsibilities, finishing second in the entire league in scoring by season's end. He was a Hart Trophy nominee and his confidence was blossoming along with his role.

This development of young talent, along with the Penguins' acquisition of Marian Hossa from the Atlanta Thrashers, put the team in position to make a deep post-season run. They finished the regular season on top of the Atlantic Division and were only two points behind the number one seeded, Montreal Canadiens.

With another year of experience under their belts, the Penguins met the Ottawa Senators in the opening round for the second consecutive year. The team looked sharp from the get-go and went on to sweep the Senators in four games. The Penguins' second round opponent was the New York Rangers, who they also defeated fairly easily. In the third round, the team met the

Philadelphia Flyers and were able to defeat them in only five games.

The series victory against the Flyers marked the Penguins first Stanley Cup Finals berth in over fifteen years. Their opponent, the Detroit Red Wings, were considered the favorite to win it all by most "experts" around the league. Detroit got off to a red-hot start and absolutely dominated the Penguins in the first two games, shutting them out completely - winning by scores of 4-0 and 3-0.

Game 3 was different, as Sidney scored two goals and the Penguins were able to take a 3-2 victory to keep the series competitive. However, the Red Wings bounced right back and took the victory in Game 4, giving them an overwhelming 3-1 series lead. After the Penguins kept their hopes alive by taking Game 5, the Red Wings finished the series off in Game 6.

The series finished much differently than how it started, with the last four games all relatively competitive and wildly entertaining. Nonetheless, it was a disappointing end for the Penguins, who had their hopes set on bringing the Stanley Cup back to Pittsburgh. Sidney totaled twenty-seven points for the entirety of the playoffs, tied with Henrik Zetterberg for the playoff scoring lead. For the regular season, Sidney was able to score 72 points in the 53 games that he played in.

Sidney and the Penguins entered the 2008-09 season with high expectations and sights set on coming through in the Stanley Cup Finals this time around. In October, Sidney accomplished the benchmark of 100 goals scored, 200 assists, and 300 total points for his career. In an interesting sequence of events, the benchmark was reached by Sidney assisting Malkin on his own 200th career point. As a result, the team's trainer cut the puck in half so that both stars could have a piece of the achievement.

Sidney experienced a relatively injury-free season and was able to develop great chemistry with his teammates as their offense became one of the best in recent NHL history. He finished the regular season with a total of 103 points, including 70 assists - a big part in Evgeni Malkin receiving the Art Ross Trophy for the year. By this point, Sydney was becoming one of the most respected players in all of the league, especially because of his unselfish play and ability to mentor his teammates - something that not all superstars are able to do effectively.

The team finished the regular season with 45 wins and ended up second in the division, good enough to make the Stanley Cup Playoffs. The Penguins defeated the Philadelphia Flyers in the first round and met the Washington Capitals in the second round. The match-up was heavily promoted by the NHL, as it featured a great deal of star-power and personalities. Ovechkin, Sidney, and Malkin were considered three of the best offensive players in the entire league, finishing as the top three point scorers in all of the NHL for the previous two seasons.

Fans were in for a treat, as the series certainly lived up to the hype. The Capitals took the first two games of the series, after Sidney and Ovechkin each scored three goals in both of their first career playoff hat tricks in Game 2. In an unexpected turn of events, the Penguins flipped the momentum completely around in Game 3 and won each of the next three games, taking a 3-2 series lead. After the Capitals took Game 6, the Penguins won Game 7, thanks in part to a two goal effort by Sidney.

The Penguins met the Carolina Hurricanes in the last round of the Eastern Conference bracket and handled them fairly easily. They swept the Hurricanes in four games and outscored them by a total of twenty to nine. The victory meant that the Penguins would be matched up in the Stanley Cup Finals against the Detroit Red Wings for the second consecutive year.

Although the Penguins desperately wanted to get the series off to a dramatically different start then the year before, things did not turn out that way. In fact, it was deja vu for the Penguins, who found themselves in a hole, down 0-2 after the first two games. The Red Wings were focusing their defensive efforts on neutralizing Sidney's play-making abilities and it was very effective, as he did not score in the first two games. However, the Penguins were determined to avoid the same fate and battled to change the momentum of the series in Game 3.

The Penguins took Game 3 after Sidney assisted to Sergei Gonchar for the game-winning goal. However, Sidney truly asserted his dominance in Game 4, most notably when he scored a goal on a 2-on-1 break with the score tied at two apiece. Only a few minutes afterwards, Sidney assisted an absolutely beautiful pass to Tyler Kennedy for a goal to put the Penguins up by two. Sidney's clutch performance helped the Penguins tie the series up at 2-2, avoiding the dreaded 3-1 deficit that they found themselves in the previous year.

After the Red Wings took Game 5, the Penguins showed their resilience once again in a Game 6 victory. Game 6 featured an incredible performance of goal-tending by Chris Osgood, who was snagging shot after shot by the Penguins offense. However, Marc-Andre Fleury was holding his own on the other side, keeping the game within striking distance the entire time. Ultimately, the Penguins were able to score a goal in both the second and third periods, giving them a 2-1 victory in a game for the ages.

Because of the dramatic build-up of the games in the series, as well as the big names involved,

Game 7 was the most watched hockey game since the 1973 Stanley Cup Finals. The game was played on the Red Wings' home ice and it was another closely-fought battle, resulting in a 2-1 victory for the Penguins.

The series win avenged their heartbreaking loss of the previous year and marked a huge victory for the city of Pittsburgh and the Penguins organization - a franchise that had been dealing with so many heartaches and let-downs during the decade. For Sidney, he became the youngest captain to ever win a Stanley Cup and headed into the off-season for a nice, relaxed recovery after suffering a knee injury in Game 7.

After an off-season of celebration and recovery, Sidney returned in typical form for the 2009-10 season. He finished the year tied for the league lead in goals scored with Steven Stamkos, earning the Rocket Richard Trophy. Sidney finished with 109 total points, enough to tie him for second in the league in points with friendly rival Alex Ovechkin. Sidney's focus on scoring more goals showed his diversity as one of the great offensive players of his generation, able to distribute or score at the elite level, all depending on what the team's needs are at the time.

The Penguins made the Stanley Cup Playoffs once again, but were defeated in the second round by the Montreal Canadiens in a closely-fought seven games series. For the playoffs, Sidney totaled nineteen points in only thirteen games.

In the 2010 Winter Games held in Vancouver, Sidney was a representative for Team Canada. The team was absolutely stacked with talent, featuring many NHL All-Stars, as well as a host of young players under the age of twenty-five. Because of so much youth, Sidney was considered one of the respected leaders of the team.

Team Canada went on to blow the Russians out in the first game of the medal round, by a score of 7-3. This was followed by a closely-fought game against Slovakia in which the Canadians emerged victorious. Team Canada then went on to meet the Americans in the Gold Medal game. The game was highly-anticipated and one of the most viewed events of all the 2010 Winter Games.

After Canada opened a two-goal lead in the second period, the Americans were able to cut the lead in half. After an exciting back and forth during the third period, Zach Parise of USA was able to score a late goal to send the game into overtime.

Sidney's clutch gene came through once again, as he took over the overtime period by aggressively taking on three defenders in an offensive push. After his shot was redirected by Ryan Miller, the American goalie, Sidney converted on a pass from Jarome Iginla. The goal finished the overtime period and marked an end to a dramatic Gold Medal game.

Upon entering the Winter Games, most Canadian hockey fans felt that the only missing part of Sidney's career was him being a catalyst in winning a gold medal for his country. Not only did he bring home a gold medal and cement his position as one of the greatest Canadian hockey players of all-time, but Sidney did it in his typical style - coming through in the clutch. Because of his dazzling display on the ice as part of team Canada, Sidney was recognized as the undisputed top Canadian hockey player.

He received his third Canadian Male Athlete of the Year award, otherwise known as the Lionel Conacher Award, in 2010 after getting the nod from the Canadian Press in 2007 and 2009. In those two years, Sidney was also awarded with the Lou Marsh Memorial Trophy as Canada's top athlete.

Sidney's 2010-11 season consisted of a 25-game point streak, beginning in early November and ending in late December. He was absolutely dominant during that period, assisting on 24 goals, scoring 27 goals, and even posting three hat-tricks. He was a lock for the All-Star Game once again, this time accompanied by three other teammates - Malkin, Fleury, and Letang. Unfortunately, neither Sidney nor Malkin were able to play in the game due to injuries.

Sidney had suffered concussion-like symptoms after multiple hits to the head only a few days prior to the selection. Upon further evaluation, it was determined that Sidney would need some time away from the game to fully recover. He spent the remainder of the year recovering and was unable to make a return for the Penguins' Stanley Cup Playoffs run.

Another blow to the Penguins' Stanley Cup hopes came when Evgeni Malkin suffered a torn MCL and ACL, causing him to also miss the remainder of the season. With their top two scorers ruled out, the Penguins were looking towards the next season. Sidney still finished the year as the team's leading scorer, at 66, even though he did not play in the team's last forty-one games. He set an interesting record for the season, as he played in the fewest games ever by a team's leading scorer.

After missing the first twenty games of the 2011-12 season in recovery for his concussion, Sidney made his season debut on November 21st, 2011. He showed little rust as he scored two goals and dished out two assists in a 5-0 victory. Sidney went on to play another seven games before his concussion-like symptoms re-appeared.

He returned again in mid-March against the New York Rangers, recording an assist in the team's victory. Despite not being able to play as much as he would have wanted to, Sidney almost averaged a 2:1 point to game ratio, showing that he was extremely productive when he was on the ice. Furthermore, he reached the 600 career point mark during the season.

Most importantly, Sidney was able to return for the Penguins' playoff run. The team had been performing well and they entered the post-season as one of the teams that could potentially win it all. The Penguins faced the much-improved Philadelphia Flyers in the first round of the playoffs, eventually falling into a 3-0 hole. After the Penguins took the next two games, they lost Game 6 to the Flyers.

As the Penguins headed into the off-season, management had a decision to make about Sidney and the future of their franchise. In the end, they offered Sidney a $104 million contract covering the span of twelve years. Such a long-term contract showed that the franchise wanted to keep Sidney with them for the long-haul and were not afraid of his concussion-like symptoms or a decline in production, as much as they appreciated what he brought to the franchise, both on and off the ice.

Because of the 2012-13 NHL Lockout, the following regular season did not start until

January. Sidney was a part of the negotiation process, as part of the NHLPA meetings with the owners. He kept himself sharp during the prolonged collective-bargaining process, playing in exhibition games along with other NHL players. Along with many other players, he even considered signing with teams of other leagues, primarily in Europe. However, in the end he decided to stay in North America and continue to keep his skills sharp through intense practice.

Sidney got off to a hot start in January, leading the league in scoring, at 31 points, over the first twenty-one games. He kept his momentum going throughout March, as he scored 25 points in only fifteen games, leading the Penguins to an undefeated record during that time. However, a slapshot caught Sidney in the mouth on March 30th in a game against the New York Islanders, leading to a diagnosis of a broken jaw.

The damage was severe and along with a shattered jaw, Sidney had lost a few teeth from the shot. After Sidney underwent multiple sessions of reconstructive dental surgery, he was forced to miss the last twelve games of the regular season. He would have most likely finished with the league lead in points had he not suffered the injury, as he was only four points behind Martin St. Louis upon season's end.

The Penguins went on to make the post-season and Sidney made a return for the second game in the first round against the New York Islanders - the same team that he faced in the game where his jaw was injured. Sidney scored two goals in the game but the Penguins went on to lose by a score of 3-2. The Penguins ended up winning the series in six games and Sidney was credited with nine points in the five games that he played in.

The Penguins faced the Ottawa Senators in the second round of the playoffs. Sidney went on to record a hat-trick in a Game 2 victory, helping the Penguins take momentum of the series. The Penguins went on to win the series four games to one, and Sidney finished with two assists to go along with four goals scored.

Most experts around the league believed that the match-up between the Penguins and the Boston Bruins in the Eastern Conference Finals consisted of the best two teams in the conference. The Penguins were hoping to make it back to the Stanley Cup Finals after a few years away from glory, but they were met by a force of a goaltender by the name of Tuukka Rask.

Rask, the Finnish goaltender of the Boston Bruins, put on a display for the ages, only allowing two goals in the entirety of the series. He stopped 134 out of 136 shots on goal, an incredible mark of 98.5%. Despite the great effort put forth by the Penguins' offense, Rask was just on one of the best streaks that the league had seen in quite awhile. The Bruins went on to sweep the Penguins in four games, earning a berth to the Stanley Cup Finals.

Sidney's 2013-14 season was relatively free of injury, as he was able to play in eighty games for the first time since the 2009-10 campaign. His total of 68 assists and 36 goals was among the best in the league. The season also marked the first time that Sidney finished atop the rankings in total assists. His total of 104 points was also a league high, earning him the Art Ross Trophy for the second time in his career.

The Penguins were able to finish the year in second place in the Eastern Conference standings, just behind the Boston Bruins. The team's first round match-up was against the Columbus Blue Jackets. Despite a series where Sidney was not able to produce his usual impressive stat-line, the Penguins emerged victorious in six games for the opportunity to play the New York Rangers in the second round. After a valiant effort against the Rangers in the first six games of the series, the Penguins were unable to win Game 7.

Despite not fulfilling his desire of getting back to the Stanley Cup Finals, Sidney was still able to put together a productive, full year of play. Only a few years prior, it was debated whether Sidney should even continue to play hockey due to his concussion issues. However, his hard work and determination eventually paid off for the Penguins, and their faith in him was repaid tenfold. For the year, Sidney was one of the finalists for the Hart Memorial Trophy, along with Claude Giroux and Ryan Getzlaf.

Sid the Kid continued his brilliant performance in the 2013-14 season. In the 80 games he played in, his most since the 2009-10 season, Sidney scored 36 goals and had 104 total points. He also led the league with 68 assists for the first time in his career. His offensive prowess was recognized once more with his second Art Ross Trophy. He won the Hart Memorial Trophy after being named as one of the top three finalists, along with Philadelphia Flyers' Claude Giroux and Ryan Getzlaf of the Anaheim Mighty Ducks, for the fourth time in his career. The last time Sidney won the trophy was after the 2006-07 season. He also won the Ted Lindsay Award, his third.

As for the team, the Penguins didn't fare as well. They held on to second place in the Eastern Conference with the Boston Bruins leading the pack. The Penguins faced the Columbus Blue Jackets in the first round of the playoffs. Pittsburgh prevailed despite a zero goal performance by Sidney. They went on to battle the New York Rangers in the second round.

The first two games were held in Pittsburgh. Sidney again failed to score in Game 1 of the series, which the Penguins dropped. He was finally able to score a goal in the second game, helping his team tie the series. Pittsburgh won Games 3 and 4 at Madison Square Garden. The Rangers bounced back by taking the next two games. With the series tied at 3-3, a deciding Game 7 was needed. Unfortunately for the Penguins, the Rangers stole the series.

Losing the Eastern Conference semifinal round series after being the higher seed and claiming the first two games didn't sit well with ownership. The fact that the team had been eliminated from the playoffs by a lower seed for the fifth consecutive time made matters worse. General Manager Ray Shero was fired and replaced with Jim Rutherford who once held the same title with the Carolina Hurricane franchise. Rutherford then let go of Dan Bylsma and hired Mike Johnston as the team's new head coach.

The 2014-15 NHL season saw Sidney scoring his 800th career point and 300th career goal. He was the sixth fastest player to reach 800 points with "The Great One" leading the pack. In fact, Gretzky holds the record for the fewest games to reach 1,000 points with 424. A few more years under his belt and Crosby may join Gretzky, former Penguins Lemieux and Jagr, and 80 other members of the elite 1,000-point club.

Hockey legend Gordie Howe is at the top spot with 1,850 points to his name.

The season started off great for the Penguins but the team was riddled with injuries. They were tasked the second wild card position, allowing them to compete in the Eastern Conference playoffs. Pittsburgh was again eliminated in five games by the Rangers in the first round, even after Sidney won Game 2 courtesy of his two goals. Sidney capped the season with 84 points behind Jamie Benn with 87 and John Tavares with 86 points. Benn went on to win the Art Ross Trophy after scoring four points in his last game of the regular season. Sidney ended up fifth in the race for the Hart Trophy.

Sidney represented his country once more during the offseason. He was named captain of Canada's Olympic hockey team, which won the gold meal over Sweden at the Sochi Olympics.

The Penguins made a number of drastic moves that completely changed the look of their roster for the 2015-16 NHL season. Gone were forwards Kasperi Kapanen and Nick Spalding, and defenseman Scott Harrington. In their place, forwards Tyler Biggs and Phil Kessel. Also included in the lineup was the former Toronto Maple Leafs defenseman Tim Erixon.

Management also sent a 2016 third round pick to the Edmonton Oilers for defenseman Justin

Schultz. Forward David Perron and defenseman Adam Clendening have also changed addresses, going from Pittsburgh to Anaheim in exchange for forward Carl Hagelin.

Penguins forward Patric Hornqvist will welcome Hagelin, whom he trains with during the offseason, with open arms. Matia Marcantuoni and Sergei Plotnikov were sent to the Arizona Coyotes in separate trades. Even their coach got the boot in the middle of the recently concluded season.

Sidney struggled to score in most parts of the season. In the first 29 games, he only scored six goals. A far cry from the time he could score that many in just a single game. This had led some to believe that Sidney is on his last leg. The rollercoaster roster changes and the firing of head coach Johnston further put a damper on their season.

The Penguins were 15-10-3 when Johnston was let go. However, since their new coach Mike Sullivan arrived, the Penguins have gone on a scoring frenzy. Sidney punctuated that sudden resurgence with a three-goal performance on February 2nd.

That was Sidney's first hat trick in five years and the ninth of his career. He garnered three points a few days later to break the 900-point barrier. Those three points not only made him the 10th fastest player to reach 900, but they also paved the way for a comeback win over the Florida Panthers.

He was named the First Star of the Month of March after he scored at least a point in 15 of 16 games. The following month, Sidney came up with his 600th assist, which helped the Penguins reach the Stanley Cup Playoffs once more.

Pittsburgh gained home ice advantage after Sidney won the game against the Washington Capitals in overtime. He was voted by his fellow Penguins as the team MVP after posting 36 goals and 85 points. It also helped a lot that Sidney played well on the other side of the ice. In fact, Senior Advisor of Hockey Operations Scotty Bowman, one of the greatest coaches in NHL history, believes that Sidney should be considered for the Frank J. Selke Trophy, the award given to the best defensive forward.

Sidney later played for Team Canada at the IIHF World Championship. When the team struck gold, Sidney finally became a member of the prestigious Triple Gold Club. What's even more impressive is that he is the only player in the Triple Gold Club to captain all three of his teams that have won the Stanley Cup, IIHF World Championship, and an Olympic Gold Medal. And he is far from finished. Sidney plans to play again for Team Canada at the 2016 World Cup of Hockey.

Sidney currently has 938 points, 338 goals, 600 assists and 707 games to his credit. He's on track to reach the 1,000 point plateau before he calls it quits. At 28 years old, he is still relatively young, especially if you consider how long some of the legends of the game have stayed on the ice.

Gordie Howe hung up his skates for the second and final time in 1980 at age of 52 while Chris Chelios was 48 when he retired in 2010. Lemieux was 40 when he called it a career in 2005, while former teammate and friend Jagr is still scoring goals at 44 years old for the Panthers.

Chapter 3:

Personal Adult Life

Sidney lived with the Lemieux family from the years 2005 to 2010 before purchasing his own home in the spring of 2010. However, he bought an off-season home in Halifax, Nova Scotia in June of 2006. Sidney has a biography out by the name of *Sidney Crosby: Taking the Game by Storm*, which goes behind the scenes of one of the most hyped hockey phenoms since Wayne Gretzky.

Sidney also posed shirt-less for *GQ Magazine* in a feature about him during November of 2005. Among other notable media appearances, he was nominated as one of the "100 Most Influential People" of 2007 by *Time Magazine*. Additionally, Sidney appeared in a documentary by the name of *Pond Hockey*, where he discusses his experiences with the game.

Sidney has been endorsed by sports giant, Reebok, for the majority of his professional career. In 2007, he even helped to design a fashion line. Three years later, Sidney signed the richest endorsement deal of any player in the history of the National Hockey League. The deal he signed with Reebok pays him $1.5 million per year. In addition to Reebok, Sidney is also sponsored by Gatorade, Tim Hortons, and Bell.

An interesting aside regarding Sidney's jersey number is that he chose the number 87 because it reflects his birth date, 8/7/87. Also, Sidney's nickname of "Sid the Kid" was first given to him because he was always the best kid on the ice. "Sid the Kid" was then used because he became a phenom in Canada at such a young age. Ever since then, the nickname has stuck with him.

It was also during his younger years that Sidney first manifested his intense character. His father Troy knows very well where Sidney got his emotional side. Father and son share the passion for the sport and in other facets of their lives. Their hatred for losing shows up when Sidney plays. There are times that media pundits see him as a "whiner" but Troy simply dismisses that notion and explains that Sidney "wears his heart on his sleeve."

Malkin was drafted second overall in 2004 by the Penguins but had issues with the transfer from his Russian club. He and Sidney finally played together in 2006 and have since been connected to each other. When Sidney went down with an injury, Malkin stepped up and showed why he was drafted so high by the franchise. Since then, the offensive arsenal of the Penguins has never been better.

While Sidney has seen some slow starts in the past few seasons, it is hard to see a Penguins franchise without him. However, if ever that trade materializes, you know that Sidney will take it like a true professional.

Obviously, his heart is with the city of Pittsburgh but it beats even harder for the sport. Wherever he goes or whether he stays to play out his career, it will always be about hockey for this passionate professional.

Chapter 4:

Philanthropic/Charitable Acts

Sidney has used his superstardom for more than just earning a nice income and becoming a hockey legend. He has made it a point to help give back through charitable acts. Sid the Kid believes that kids are innocent and deserve a "chance to live their life". This concept led to the creation of the "Sidney Crosby Foundation" in 2009.

The foundation's main goal is to provide financial support to charities that can provide opportunities for underprivileged children, especially those who are suffering from some kind of medical condition, kids with family issues, and those struggling to survive financially. One of the notable donations that Sidney has made, was to give his entire 2010 Olympic Games winnings to the foundation. He reached an agreement with Bell Canada, that they would match his donation.

The Sidney Crosby Foundation has also started the Sidney Crosby Hockey School. The camp, located in Cole Harbour, is open to boys and girls who wish to learn the ins and outs of hockey. They undergo different on-ice, off-ice, and even dry-land activities that will help them develop their skills. The participants learn from a number of hockey experts, including former and current NHL players and coaches. The net proceeds from the registration fees and other money that comes in are given to the Sidney Crosby Foundation.

The foundation has also contributed to the Breakfast Program of Canada. They have helped out with the breakfast program of the Colonel John Stuart Elementary School. This is made possible by the Halifax Regional School Board, a partner of the foundation.

Sidney not only lent his name to his foundation and hockey school, but he has also partnered with his first ever hockey league – the Timbits Minor Hockey League -- as its official ambassador. Sidney shot an advertising campaign in 2007 with a handful of Timbits players that promoted Timbits Hockey. The ad was titled "The First Goal is Having Fun".

Sidney has also donated hockey equipment to multiple minor league hockey teams in his home province of Nova Scotia. The teams were not able to pay for the necessary equipment and

Sidney decided to help make the young boys' desire of playing hockey come true. As someone who knows the struggle of gathering the necessary funds for a youngster's hockey equipment, he has gone above and beyond to help provide opportunities to kids who would otherwise have to call it quits on the sport.

Sidney's contributions are not just limited to giving financial assistance. He has even visited the Children's Hospital in Pittsburgh multiple times. Along with some of his Penguins' teammates, Sidney was able to brighten up the lives of many kids who are suffering from illnesses that were out of their control. Additionally, during his time with the Penguins, Sidney has purchased a suite for different families to come enjoy a Penguins game first-hand.

He is also a frequent participant in other Penguins' charitable events, particularly the Mario Lemieux Foundation. Sidney and teammate Evgeni Malkin have purchased a couple of luxury suites at the CONSOL Energy Center, the Penguins' home rink, to accommodate different foundations. Children from such groups are welcomed into the suites where they can watch the Penguins play for free. They also receive gifts from Sidney and Malkin.

In previous years, Sidney has done similar acts of purchasing suites to be used by charitable groups for a whole season. Sidney purchased a suite at the Mellon Arena which has hosted events such as the "Hockey Fights Cancer Awareness Night" where children from the Make-A-Wish Foundation were treated to a Penguins game. Other foundations such as Tickets For Kids, The Caring Place, the Boys & Girls Club, and Variety – The Children's Charity have also used the suites before.

The D.T. Watson Home for Autistic Children, The Bradley Center, Pathfinder School, Special Olympics of Allegheny County, and The Depaul School for Hearing and Speech are some of the other groups that benefited from Sidney's desire to help children and the community.

Sidney has also participated in other charitable work for foundations such as *Big Brothers Big Sisters, The Bone Marrow Transplant/Oncology Unit of UPMC Shadyside,* and *Make-A-Wish*. He has also helped re-develop a lounge for patients at the IWK Health Center in Halifax and it has rejuvenated the spirit of the center.

The new lounge is meant to provide opportunities to socialize for teenagers that are dealing with an illness, who can now connect with their peers in enjoyable ways. These teenagers can participate in group activities such as birthday parties, arts and crafts, and even cooking. Sidney was personally there during different parts of the refurbishing process, connecting with the patients in person. He did much of this while recovering from his concussion-like symptoms.

Sidney has also listed a number of his jerseys up for auction, with the proceeds going towards different causes. One of his jerseys was sold for over $22,000 with proceeds going towards youth hockey programs and the 2004 Indian Ocean Earthquake relief efforts. Another jersey was sold for over $21,000 with proceeds going to relief efforts for the Hurricane Katrina disaster. An auction held by the NHL to benefit "Hockey Fights Cancer" was able to sell Sidney's 2007 All-Star Game jersey for over $47,000!

Sidney has even been publicly recognized for his great deal of charitable work, including being awarded the Mark Messier Leadership Award by the NHL in two different seasons. The award is meant to highlight a player that is a leader on the ice while also being a leader in the community and just an overall great role-model for others.

Chapter 5:

Legacy, Potential & Inspiration

Even though Sidney is still young in his career and hopefully has a long list of seasons left in front of him, there is no doubt that he has already developed a legacy for himself. As a player, he is clearly one of the most offensively gifted athletes that he league has ever seen.

His talent, combined with a quarter decade of hard work, has given him the ability to deal with practically any type of defensive strategy than can be applied. Because he has been the target of defenses for so long, he is wise beyond his years.

Sidney's ability to play at a great pace while still keeping his composure and technical skills top-notch is what allows him to make plays on the fly and provide those highlight plays that fans have come to love. Additionally, his unselfish style and desire to set up his teammates, even when he could probably take the shot himself, makes others give high praise on his behalf.

He does not disappear when defenders get rough, making it a point to establish his presence on the ice. This combination of finesse and power is second-to-none in the sport. Mentally, he seems to be in control of the puck, not letting the big moment or other players get into his head. While he can force the issue when the game is close and his team needs a goal, he prefers to let the game come to him and capitalize when he sees an opportunity.

His powerful build, specifically his strong legs, gives him a great first step and allows him to keep a strong base during collisions. However, all of this talent and ability is nothing without a strong will to win and leadership skills. Sidney has proven that he can be a captain of a championship team and mentor younger (and older) players when they are looking for guidance. Despite his position as a transcendent celebrity, Sidney continues to work as hard as someone just trying to earn a roster spot on an NHL team.

An unfortunate negative aspect about being a transcendent athlete such as Sidney, or those that have come before him like Wayne Gretzky, is that you are subject to a great deal of jealousy and envy by your peers. Sidney has had to deal with this his whole career and has handled it rather well. Even as a youth hockey player, Sidney has dealt with verbal abuse, other players attempting to injure him, and even pre-game taunting.

Sidney has even recalled being taunted by opposing teams' parents during his youth hockey days, going so far as to not put his jersey on until just before stepping on the ice, so that he would not be recognized and could avoid verbal abuse in the off-time between tournament games. The over-the-top issues he faced as a youngster was even one of the factors for him deciding to enroll in Shattuck-Saint Mary's hockey program for a year.

His per game production is among the highest in league history and his teammates and coaches have commented about how the game feels easier when number 87 is out there on the ice. He has overcome serious concussion issues, a shattered jaw, and multiple other obstacles on his way, and amazingly shows very little rust each time he comes back - thanks to his incredible drive and work ethic.

Sidney will always be compared to the greatest players of all-time, such as Gretzky, Lemieux, and Bobby Orr. He may or may not live up to some people's amazingly high expectations of him, but he is certainly an example that we can all learn from. Even though he is one of the greatest players statistically, most people love him for his intangibles.

He, along with Alex Ovechkin, are two of the main driving factors in keeping the sport of hockey relevant amongst casual fans. Because the sport is so technical and not played in all parts of the world, it needs incredible offensive players like Sidney to keep it in the mainstream eye. Especially come playoff time, you can count on Sid the Kid to draw ratings for the NHL.

Conclusion

Hopefully this book was able to help you gain inspiration from the life of Sidney Crosby, one of the best players currently playing in the National Hockey League.

The rise and fall of a star is often the cause for much wonder. But most stars have an expiration date. In hockey, once a star player reaches his mid- to late-thirties, it is often time to contemplate retirement. What will be left in people's minds about that fading star?

In Sidney's case, people will remember how he led a franchise in their journey towards a championship. He will be remembered as the guy who plucked his franchise from obscurity, helped them build their image, and honed his own image along the way.

Sidney has also inspired so many people because he is the star who never fails to connect with fans and give back to the less fortunate. Noted for his ability to impose his will on any game, he is a joy to watch on the ice. Last but not least, he's remarkable for remaining simple and firm with his principles in spite of his immense popularity.

Hopefully you've learned some great things about Sidney in this book and are able to apply some of the lessons that you've learned to your own life! Good luck in your journey!

Manufactured by Amazon.ca
Bolton, ON

25461616R00037